Me, You, Us & T

By Cleave Armstrong

For Karl

x

Copyright © 2016 by Cleave Armstrong

All rights reserved. This book or any portion thereof
may not be reproduced or used in any manner whatsoever
without the express written permission of the publisher
except for the use of brief quotations in a book review.

The writings in this book were first started over thirty years ago. In care from the age of seven, I first started writing as an attempt to escape from environments that I had no control over, but it also became a useful way to explore and express my own frustrations.

In the beginning, everything I wrote was from a personal perspective, but as the years rolled on, the more people I met and the more stories I heard that inspired me. So I decided to write not just for myself but for all those other people too. This encouraged me to try writing from perspectives other than my own, to empathise and see things from another point of view.

The issues addressed in this work are wide-ranging but all of them are original and true. Some you may find distressing, others perhaps humorous and some may be difficult to understand, but all are related to individuals and sadly some of those individuals are no longer with us.

What I'm hoping that the reader will find, is the reality that I've tried to portray. Too many people go through life expressing that they care and understand one individuals situation from another, but do any of us really understand? I hope that when you have read this, that maybe you will understand a little more and spend that little bit more time to read between the lines.

I dread to think what course my life would have taken or where I would have ended up, without the people who were my inspiration and the writings that they enabled me to create. So I would like to use this space to thank them wholeheartedly and dedicate this book of poetry to them all.

-Cleave

Contents:

Skins	9
Playing	10
Scars	12
Blood-rush & Spoons	15
Friends	16
Fears	18
Beer Cans & Cardboard	20
Dancer	21
Spider's Water	23
Creaking Doors	25
Brushes	27
Monuments	28
Playing With Matches	30
Blackened Sun	31
Pitmen's Blood	33
Angels	35
Rainbows	37
Mirrors	39
Thoughts & Dreams	41
Red-eyed Monster	43
God's Cloud	45

Because Of You	47
True	48
Doors	50
Poor	52
Smile	53
Kicking Pebbles	55
Boat By The Sea	57
Nothing At All	58
Fresh Start	60
Maybe	61
Broken	63
Sweet Maidens	65
Will	67
Karma	68
Jack's Visit	70
Children	72
Cold Love	73
Empty	76
Snake's Garden	78
Answers	80
Fate	82
Lost Sons	84
Shallow Dreams	85
Tears	87

Cosmic Mate	89
On The Canvas	91
Wish	93
The Jester	95
Voices	96
Remember Me	98
Everywhere	100
Minds Existence	101
Distant Lands	103
Golden Waters	105
Moments	106
Kiss	107
Hearts Cannot Be Shared	108
Expectations	109
Your Song	111
Joyful Amazing Kind Everlasting	113
Running	114
Special Someone	116
What Place?	118
Shoes	119
Done More	121
Truth Or Lies	123
Willow Tree	125
Jollies	127

Barriers	130
Smiles	132
Weaker	133
Really Love You	135
Wings Of Gold	137
Stronger	139
Solvent Dreams	141
Down	142
Lost	144
Bang Shout Bang	146
Shackles	147
Think	149
Autumn Leaves	151
Cold Blood	152
Helentree	154
First Night	155
Faces	157
Your Eyes	159
Skin Deep	161
Segregated	163
Day Trip	164
Monster	166
Patches	167
Happier Song	169

Touch	170
Along The Way	172
Campfire Nights	174
Pretty Once	175
Corridors	177
Place Of Wonder	178
Crying Sky	179
Protector	180
Tick Tock	181

Skins

It's always the same where ever we roamed...
whether with someone or whether alone...
Paki they call us, niggers or coons!
Why?...Because our skins not like their own?

"It's our country" they tell us, "go back to your own",
"don't talk to no one", "leave our women alone!"
Why do they this? What have we done wrong?
We are just like you are, made of flesh, blood and bones.

I would die for this country, I'd protect it alone.
I'd spill all my blood on it's streets and it's stones.
I'd walk in to battle, I'd fight by their sides.
I'd do all in my power to save their white hides!...

But it would still be the same,
wherever we roamed...
Paki they would call us, niggers, or coons!...
Why...because our skin is not like their own.

Playing

To sail back in time,
I flow at a time that I was young,
of climbing trees and scrumping.
And the pit-lifts played their song,
the thundering of the wagons
as they carry their black gold.
And pop and crisps
and Blackpool trips
and bingo for the old.

Of assemblies in the mornings
and prayers at end of day,
then to meet up by the school gates:
to watch the cock of the schools display.
To wander in the pit canteen,
as the staff they drink their tea...
to help myself to Wagon Wheels
and pit men's meals
and then to run away.

To meet up by the sand bank,
the stony hill or by the ditch.
To ride on the back of motorbikes,

along the fireman's track
or to watch who rides the highest hill,
in the valley round the back.
To play trekking in the woodlands.
To nest amongst the trees, to run and trip and fall...
and graze your grubby knees.
To gaze upon the hoppers:
choosing rock, from brick to stones.
To ride upon it's rubber belly -
until the miners start to moan.

The rumbling in your tummy,
the dryness in your mouth,
to the closing of the days curtains
the setting of the sun.
It's home that we go...to the distant calling of your mom.
To sausage, eggs, chips and beans
and a glass of council pop.
Then it's up the wooden hills we go,
you don't even have a wash.

Scars

Wet and miserable, soggy and wet.
Not a glimpse of sunshine, not one sunset.
Cold to the bones, my clothes are soaking wet.
My hands are cold and shivering,
I can't catch my breath,
My tents like a river - at least two foot deep.
My woods not for burning.
My fires all but lost.
There's rats in my cook tent, along with the fox
and the magpie it heckles me - it thinks I've lost the plot!

The sun gives me no comfort.
The nights bring the cold,
Along with some locals...
pissed up and can't go home!
I came here for a reason, a point I had to make.
But fifty two days in...I still haven't had a break.
It's rained for forty eight of those,
I've lost two stones in weight!
Yet the locals have fed me, they've been so very great,
supporting me in this madness,
this protest I had to make.

My friends have been supportive,
though some I've had to ditch!
As they showed no respect...
to where they have a piss!
But battle on I must do,
I have to make a stand,
stand up to these capitalists,
strewn across the lands!
See as common as they see me,
important though I'm not,
I will not be backed into a corner,
my gob you won't keep shut!

And I will leave no stones unturned,
I will not be left forgot!
And I shall not be ignored,
I will fight with all I've got!
And you will fall to your knees
and accept that wrong - I'm not!
See you can't ignore the people
and choose what you decide
as they don't fit your criteria of how they should provide!
You should be the provider, these people are yours!
And this path that they take, is decided by yours!

You said I should have nothing, entitled to 'nout',
as the life I had chosen, should leave me left out!
So why am I now, not soaking wet,
and why am I now, less of a threat!
Why have I got, what I asked for before,
Why am I allowed to have a front door!
The reasons are simple but painful for you,
you can't walk over people, just like you do.
Expect them to go away, is what you would do!
But I'm an individual, just like you are
and I did not ask for any of these scars.

Blood-rush & Spoon

Give me some brown, give me a rock,
give me some dope, give me the lot.
Give me a syringe, give me a spoon,
give me a vain, so I can fly to the moon!!
...that feels much better, that feels really good,
nothing to worry about - just a trickle of blood.
I feel really good now, I feel really strong.
I've never felt better - I'm totally stoned.

I think I'll lie down now I think I will rest,
I've never felt better this rush is the best!!
...but what is that feeling!!...why do I shake!
...I can't even move - my body it aches!!
...I need some brown, I need it real quick
...if I don't get it now I'm going to be sick!!

So give me some brown, give me a rock,
give me some dope, give me the lot.
Give me a syringe, give me a spoon,
find me that vain so I can fly to the moon!!!
...that feels much better that feels really good
...nothing to worry about, just a trickle of blood.

Friends

So where do I start with friends like mine?
Be brutally honest...or say nothing - don't complain.
So I'll just say, I know a person - no, it's several more,
who seem so very different, not normal for sure!
You have this one dude, so clever, so sure,
but when they've had a skin full;
can be brutal and a chore.
Then you've got their partner - loves them to the core!
Is it a match in heaven? I'm not really that sure.

Then you've got one of the exes, was married before...
not sure if this one's nuttier than the one before?!
But also very clever and sometimes very kind -
very quick to help their own blood,
but their trust is hard to find.
Then you've got the partner of the one that's very kind,
now they are very trustworthy,
and they've worked so very hard -
anything they promised you
would be as sure as there are stars!
but sometimes they get lonely, feel they're left behind
and their dummy they spit, they go on the piss,
and feel like leaving their vows behind!

Then comes the diamond, the opal, a treasure, a star -
the one that's so emotional, but the tightest one by far!
Then you've got the tight one's sidekick,
together they've been far,
the sidekicks very lovable and also could call a star.
But there's a chance of madness,
from the tight one's sidekick star.

Then there's the mysterious one,
the strangest one by far!
They packed up their shit, lived in Britain for a bit,
then decided to move afar!!
Now we have the lost one, yet kind and very strong -
but struggles now daily how to get along!

And now we come to me, friend of all above,
the one that's probably the craziest of all those above!
I can be somewhat wacky, pissed off, a spoilt brat.
I can talk, moan and squawk and become an utter ass!
But these friends of mine
should make a shrine,
to accept there all a pack
and no matter how weird,
screwed up and feared.
Let's not forget we all have pasts!

Fear

What was it to make you hurt me so,
why reach deep inside of me
and rip out all that's good,
to weaken me,
to close the doors to love,
to shatter all the dreams
I had to share with you my love.

To blink an eye I cry so much,
to sleep I lie awake,
to feel helpless and defenceless,
I plead no more for you to take.
I walk with hands in pockets
deep pain prevents me to look ahead,
I think, I try to understand
too big a bridge to make.

I sit with face in hands so much,
every voice I hear is yours,
and every song that falls upon my ears
is of us and all our years.
How for you to walk away in arms that don't belong.
With a face that's full of happiness

and a smile that stole my heart.
Yet I sit here broken with no idea of where to start.

I once stood tall and prominent,
for you I'd have changed the world.
I gave you everything I had,
my secrets, love and fears.
But you just walked away from me,
for reasons - you gave me none.
With a heart that's dull and crumbling,
with the fear to love no one.

Beer Cans & Cardboard

As your walking down these streets
there's all these people that we meet...
a piece of card, a woolly hat,
"please help me sir" and things like that...

And further on down these streets
there's still these people that we meet...
a little child, an elderly man
both drinking from a beer can...

And further on down these streets
there's still these people that we meet...
a cardboard box, a wooden shack
down beside the railway track...

And further on down these streets
there's still these people that we meet...
a crying child, a desperate man
just making out the best they can.

Dancer

So to wish for me to be lonely,
so to wish from me that you care.
And I will sing a song for you
and I will watch you dance.

But tempered fear is within you
and you will skip across the lands,
to dance to what I don't give you,
but to take, though I don't send.

You dance whether a sour tune,
and you will allow what is not worthy
to dance along with you,
for your purpose is to hurt me,
with the song I sing for you.

And you will champion your misgivings,
as if blind, though clearly you see,
to rip apart what's honest from the heart
and dance as it breaks and falls.

And you will dance upon it,
to its final beats.

You'll dance your song, keep dancing along...
as my song, it lies there dying.

But to remember this my dancer,
it was my song you loved to dance,
and now I am no longer
to watch your haunting dance.

You will dance no longer...
...as it was for me you cruelly danced.

Spider's Water

I sit alone and curse myself,
yet no blame is surely mine,
I bite my lip and pinch myself
and write upon the wall.
I write, I fight I bite some more
some water falls down my cheek.
There's voices that I'm listening to:
they scream and scream again.
Am I paying for some sin I've done?
A spider crawl's down my cheek to cast a web
to catch my lies, anger and deceit.

So young yet old I try to see,
should these questions come from me?
It's lonely and dark and fearful here
There's blackened skies above my head,
the thunder crashes, the lightning strikes,
I pull the hairs from out my head,
I'm cold, I'm hot - the sweats won't stop -
the lightning strikes again,
confused and lost my heart it stops...
to gently beat again.

My arms reach out I scream and shout
but not even God can hear my cries.
I whimper, I break, there's no more I can take,
is it a sin to wish to end it all?
But to be brave and strong, to keep moving along
as there's no blame that I should take,
to learn to grow - there's reasons I know,
which I had no wish to take.
But they were handed to me, given to me,
it was all I could do but to take...
but I was just a boy I accepted them like toys
believing that's what I should do.
But now I am older, braver and bolder
and a new path I have chosen to take,
I'll learn again over, over and over
new reasons I'll write on the wall,
no more fighting, no more biting,
no more water shall fall down my cheek,
and the spider that took over,
cast its web my life over
will drown from the water down my cheek.
And all the blame that I harnessed
will snap and be parted
and this new life of this man I will take.

Creaking Doors

As the day turns into night
my feelings turn to one of fright,
a good night kiss, a good night smile,
I ask my mom just stay a while.

And as she tucks me up in bed
I dread to think what lies ahead
I close my eyes, I start to pray...
"please help me Lord, in any way".

As I lie there scared to sleep,
I hear the sound of creeping feet!!
I close my eyes, I freeze with fear,
just knowing that he's coming here.

And as he walks on through my door
just like he as those nights before...
my heart it stops, I freeze with fear
just wishing that my mom was here...

And as he pulls back all the sheets
my heart beats with a faster beat,
I close my eyes, I start to cry...
my only wish that I could die!

And as the day turns into night
my feelings turn to one of fright,
a good night kiss, a good night smile,
I ask my mom just stay a while.

Brushes

Come here where I sit, pass the ghosts that sit with me.
Swear with your mouth and poke with your fingers,
paint me with your brush.
Am I the same or does the colour not suit me?
Drag me through your anger, is that colour there red?
Or is anger that makes you want to paint me?
You use your words for no purpose!
And the bristles on your brushes are weary,
no paint on my face can you give me.
And my ghosts will paint you
with your own brush -
whose bristles are weary.
So to defend myself from your arrogance!
To break the wings that you think make you fly better
and your feathers can paint me again!
So for you, to wonder I think,
with your brushes that's now become weary.
And to live or to die my paint it will dry,
your anger will never protect you!
You will wander alone with the brushes that you own
and drowned in the paint that you swallow!

Monuments

Languages floating through the skies,
to place messages upon my ears,
travelled a million miles or more,
days or even years.

Aromas float amongst the emptiness,
with a dialect of their own,
a crystal picture in the distance
lies with stars upon its face,
surrounded by a rainbow
of the earth's kindness and it's grace.

To stretch a thousand leagues or more,
past the islands in the sky,
my gates latch on to monuments
born across the lands.

A millennium they've resided there,
since its wet skin had seeped away,
planting their own legacy,
we're here and here to stay.

But scar's of many sleep across the lands,
it hurts to cast a glance,

the wallowing of iron horses,
rips natures skin apart.

Drowning all pleasantries,
though a million worlds apart.
But to tender grasp, reach out and feel,
surround it like a glove.

Adventure doesn't end this here,
as this does not belong to us...
as we are just their visitors here,
and to keep it they surely must.

Playing With Matches

Lost thoughts from the past come to haunt me,
much sadness and tears I can see,
fear and anger all around me...
though some happiness also I see.

Minor years of my life is like torture
cutting deep into my skin,
not really understanding
not knowing where to begin.

Growing from infant to adult,
losing the years from within...
one moment playing with matches
the next trying to force my way in.

My body it is tired and hurting,
one third of my life - it is gone.
The strength that is left within me...
just enough to keep me moving on.

There's no pleasure at all from these travels,
no pleasure at all that I see,
only regret and frustration
and the thought - "Why did this happen to me?".

Blackened Sun

For gentle reason I love.
For pain of virtue, I walk alone.
My way is that no comfort comes,
less hastened for my way in life,
as I stand in black rains shadow,
I cry alone, as I will die alone,
for power and strength will not break my walls.

For bricks to crumble in attack,
my walls are now a fortress.
To stand alone, to protect my soul in this forsaken place -
from evil prophesies that take my path.
To try to swim through careless emotions.
To try to fight with hands that do not serve me
and a conscience that's lost its way.

And my sight it will not help me,
as these darkened lands they shed no light.
I am an unknown soldier
to fight what is also unknown.
To fight ferocious battles in these darkened lands,
to spew my life's choices,
is how I've poisoned this land.

My soul it rips my uncertainty,
to cast a spell that's cold and cruel,
to blind me with its torment,
to fall, and fall again.
In these blackened lands I'm to remain,
a prisoner, along with black rains shadow,
my punishment that I dream.

I'm my own judge and juror
and my executioner I've become.
But I'm not brave enough to end this,
as a stranger to myself I've become.
But also I'm my only friend,
to fight forever...
under this blackened sun.

Pitmen's Blood

How I love to stand here,
ruling across the lands.
Seeing every home I've had
from boy until a man.
Trees of green a plenty,
fields far and wide,
looking across this landscape
brings emotion to one's eyes.

As a child I was to wander here:
adventure, hide, and play,
in the early morn I'd greet it all
and make a pact to last the day.
A million places I would go,
somewhere different every day.
The buzzards would fly above me,
asking about my day.

The hares and rabbits would hop around
while the horses ate their hay,
why the tender deer would just appear -
then gently slip away.
To make camp amongst the brambles,

the ferns and bracken bush.
This would be my castle, where I would fly my flag,
a fortress that belonged to me, protect it I surely would.

Time would travel so quickly here,
day would turn to night,
reluctantly to leave my kingdom
so much I wished to stay.
Descendents they left this mound for me,
decades of sweat and blood,
a monument to all things British,
a monument to all that's good.

When Easter falls,
the crosses stood tall
to remind us of God's gift,
I'd dance amongst their shadows
which the sun cast on the hill,
and have a chat with Jesus
and thank him for all the things he's done,
then reluctantly leave my castle,
heading back towards my home,
but not before just one play more...
on Huntington pit-men's blood.

Angels

I had a dream the other night
an angel came to me
she sat herself upon my bed
and cried so endlessly.

When I asked what was wrong
and why she seemed so sad
she said there's much in her life
that's been so very bad...

"Take my hand and come with me,
on a journey we will go
and where we've been and what you've seen
your answers you will know.

We travelled far throughout the night
and much there was too see
and oh how glad I really was
this sufferer wasn't me!!

When we returned, I was so sad
my heart was broken in two.
I couldn't believe this suffering
that this angel had gone through.

She took my hand, she lay me down,
she kissed me on the cheek,
she said she had to go now
as there's others she had to meet...

Before you go, I said to her
"your name I wish to know?
She simply turned and said to me...
be sure that you will know.

Rainbows

So you're going to give me a beating -
beat me black and blue.
Call me names, slander the same,
because I think differently to you.

You're going to get a lynch mob!
Go searching for people like me!
Hide in corners, then go and report us,
To other people like you.

My life this chose this for me,
it's something I cannot change,
as from the age of four I knew the score -
and my life's war was about to begin!

At age of six to my parents did I admit -
It's men that I wanted to kiss.
My dad found it hard, my mom was a star!
And they supported me on this.

All through school, I met some fools who would torture
and be cruel about who I wanted to kiss.
But I got older, stronger and bolder
and my friends were a special list.

And if you were on it, then you were supersonic!
Unlike the homophobic gits!
And I'll walk proudly, stand tall and be bouncy,
and be proud of who I kiss.

And you will not change me, scare or exclude me,
because I'm happy being like this.
So when you do kick me, hit me and beat me,
because you don't like who I kiss.

You made your choices, with your violence and voices,
for what purpose did you do this?!
How does it hurt you? What I decide to do!
Is it because you've got a small DICK?!!

Mirrors

To look into a mirror,
is it you, you really see,
or is someone else standing there,
someone else you'd like to be.

Do you feel your life is drifting,
across some ancient plain,
and the image that you're looking at
really needs to change.
Do you call yourself someone else,
do you wish a different life,
do you feel yourself balancing
on the edge of the sharpest knife?

Is the person looking back at you,
giving you a different name?
Are the voices in your head,
driving you insane?

Is the mirror starting to crack now,
do you feel the change within.
Eyes of blue are green now,
hair of black now red,
you've fallen off that sharpest knife,

the old you now is dead.
The mirror cracks another time,
it shatters to the floor,
you scream, you screech, you cry out loud,
you don't know who you are.

You sit amongst the shattered glass,
your sanity runs away.
There's shadows now around you,
along with shattered glass,
you've asked too much to give to you...
I loved you in the past.

Thoughts & Dreams

Comforting thoughts and dreams alike,
passing the hours from day into night
lingering endlessly to thoughts of joy,
holding them tight like a child does a toy.

Many hours have passed,
and many more they will too,
but all of my thoughts
and dreams are of you.

Sleepless nights, silent tears,
thinking of you and all our years,
I feel helpless without you...lonely and lost...
like a calf newborn or a sheep with no flock.

But I feel your presence,
your comfort, your love
and you will always be here
like the stars are above.

I often sit here looking into the abyss,
just wishing you here, just wanting your kiss,
wanting to hold you, caress you, feel,
wanting to love you so much it's unreal.

I picture you now as if here by my side...
but only to realise it's the thoughts in my mind.
I miss you my friend, much more than you know
But I have memories of you and I won't let them go.

So strong we must be
stare it straight in the face
as the time it will come
when our arms they embrace.

Red-eyed Monster

Like breaking ice - I snap and crack,
and my tongue lashing, it is frightening.
My voice it roars like thunder storms,
I beat and beat with language.

There's no control it's my control,
my outburst wants an audience.
Whether right or wrong, you'll hear my song,
I will get some emotions.

My face its mean, it changes its scenes,
like stormy clouds after sunshine.
It's angry and cruel, to stare would be a fool -
I will give you a gift from Medusa.

As my tongue it still whips - I still want my kicks
and my eyes pierce all that confronts me.
I burst and explode there's fire in my soul
and my words they are poison arrows.

They shoot who they please they
don't care who they make bleed!
From me you will get no emotions!
See my angers a beast' like Satan at least.

And I shoot my arrows while I'm burning,
And more words I set free,
much more evil from me
and I watch without tears as they slaughter!

And Medusa she joins me, and enjoys what she does see,
as my words become more fierce,
and now become like spears,
and they travel like fish in the waters!

And Medusa becomes scared,
for my words she's not prepared
and they make her feel so cold, she turns herself to stone,
as she knows my words give no quarter!

And I'll scream and shout my words I will let out,
and I'll do as I please -
bring who I like to their knees,
with love from your friend, the red eyed monster!

God's Cloud

Where for me to wonder now,
which cloud do I choose to ride,
what company to take with me,
and what to leave behind.

To sieve through my minds contents,
to abandon what's to heavy to haul,
to take with me all that's good,
and take nothing bad at all.

So to travel like a feather,
gently on the winds,
to places where I wish to go,
and be happy with what I bring.

I'll ride my cloud when the sun it sleeps,
it's brother and it's children will guide me along the way,
to travel alongside the wise nights predators
and to listen to their song.

To let my soul release itself,
to cleanse itself, engulfed in God's clean breath,
so to stand before on my judgement day to not be feared
where my afterlife will cast it's love and it's tears.

And to whoever I hold tender near will have no fear,
as God's breath has cleansed my soul,
and I travelled on my cloud alone,
with darkness as my cape;

With just the wise night predator as my companion,
while it's song it travelled faster,
to knock on gods gates,
with the message that I'm fearful;

That his gift of life I've paraded,
offered fallen angels new wing's to fly,
and to take me from my floating cloud
to a place I can never die.

Because Of You

You were always beside me
in all things that were wrong,
you gave me the support
and the strength to carry on.

Your support it is priceless,
your friendship like gold
and I will always be grateful
until the years make me old.

I owe you my life,
for all things that you've done
and I promise to thank you
at each setting of the sun.

And in the mornings,
when I wake from sleep
I'll thank you again
with the first words that I speak.

And when the time comes that I breathe my last breath
I'll thank you again - you deserve nothing less.

True

My life is cold without you,
my heart is lost it's true.
If you're not here to guide me -
to lead, to show the way.
Then I will wander aimlessly,
with no hope to find my way,

See, you are the life I live for, every single day,
and if you were not here I hasten to fear,
my life would slip away.
You're the air I need to breathe,
and your love it feeds me each day.

Your touch it brings me comfort,
your kiss allows me to sleep,
and to see you, just to look at you,
makes me feel so unique,
You are so very special,
and so important to me,
and when your here, so very near,
my heart it skips a beat.

I want you here always,
and I will always be here for you,

to wander together, to share forever,
whatever it is we seek.

For a millennium I wish this to happen,
so forever together we'd be,
with our love that's so strong, and our lives we live long,
so for a million memories we can keep.

But fools we are not, I know this,
and this is just how I dream,
yet I know it's all truth that I speak of,
and what I say of you is true.

But my soul its already tarnished,
and although what I speak of is true,
I shall remain lonely and lost,
God will not allow me to walk with you,
as you are so very special,
and other plans he has for you.

So my dream again it is ended,
and again I stand alone.
But I tell you this my sweetness -
I will hold on so very long,
to all the dreams I've had of you,
because my memories, to me they belong.

Doors

Going, going, going,
to where - I don't know,
opening doors;
revealing places I shouldn't go.
But no mind to me no mind at all,
I'll walk through every one.

I'll walk through them all.
Into the darkness, into the fire.
Into the mouth, abyss, the fear,
I keep on walking, stumbling on,
into emptiness, solitude, grievance and pain,
I keep on walking - to me there's no shame.

The distant tolling, tolling of bells
piercing my ears with screams, howls,
keep moving forward stumbling on,
breaking, breaking, breaking free -
pulling myself, away from me.

What reasons I have to walk like I do,
to show no respect, to them, to you,
but no care I have,

no care at all to the damage I cause
when I walk through these doors.
Leaving destruction the belief to trust,
leaving a stench so strong it's too much,
but I'll keep on walking,
moving on believing that I'm the only one,
I'll have everything, take what I want!!...
no one to stop me no one at all.

There's only me that resides here,
all the darkness I bring,
all the doors that I've walked through belong only to me -
there's a door for my arrogance, a door for my soul,
a door for love, a door for my hate,
a door that reveals my very own fate.

See I don't belong in this world that is yours,
I don't deserve to have sunshine and flowers,
I have no understandings, reason's or care,
like the people you are, you people out there.
So I'll keep moving forward, stumbling on -
opening doors to no flowers, no sun.

Poor

My dad's down the pub,
my mom's on the streets.
My sisters left home,
my brother just weeps!

There's no food in the cupboard,
the house is like ice.
We all sleep in the same room,
along with the mice!

The clothes we are wearing
cost ten pence or less
and everyone's living and fighting round the mess!

The neighbours ignore us -
they don't want to know.
They don't say a word,
not even hello!

I want to get away from it -
just walk out the door
...but I guess it's just life and the cost of being poor.

Smile

It's nice to see you smile today,
it's nice to see you laugh,
with all that's gone on in your life,
especially in the past.

I feel your moving on now,
moving on from a lingering past,
escaping from, all that's gone on,
it's time for you to laugh.

I will walk this with you,
all difficult steps I'll help you pass,
to carry you if I must do,
you deserve to smile and laugh.

Though your past has been your past,
and the sadness and tears have been yours,
I'm here now to fix this,
to help bring down your defensive walls.

Not everyone wants to hurt you,
not everyone can be so cruel,
there's people that want to help you,

help you, to move along.

I will be here always,
and always is a promise I'll keep,
there's nothing on this earth, to you will bring hurt,
my promise I mean to keep.

But your help I will be needing,
as without this, your walls will stand,
and no matter how much I fight and stand tough,
without this I will fall.

So together we will fight this,
together we'll break these walls
and we will be strong and no matter how long,
you will laugh and be smiling.

Kicking Pebbles

Walking down the street again,
hands in pockets head bowed in shame,
kicking pebbles - oh not again,
Worked all week - worked really hard,
it's Friday now the weekend starts.

People walk past me, dressed up for the night,
out for a laugh maybe a fight,
I just keep walking, head to the ground,
cursing myself "not even a pound!".

What to say this time!
My excuses are few,
every week something different,
every week something new.

Maybe I lost it,
maybe I was robbed!
Maybe I should run away
and make my peace with God.

I'm nearing my home now,
I have to go in,

let's be really quiet...
I hope they're not in.

Walk through the kitchen,
go slowly up the stairs,
to sit in my bedroom,
just me and my despairs.

It won't happen next week, never again,
fed up of this problem, fed up of this pain,
fed up of lying, fed up of the shame,
fed up of every Friday feeling exactly the same.

But many times I have said it, so many promises I've made,
trying to find excuses why I haven't been paid!
But when Friday comes it will be exactly the same,
hands in pockets head to the ground,
kicking pebbles - not even a pound.

Boat by the sea

What do you really think when I speak of my life?
What are your pictures of my house and home life?

Children in nappies unchanged for too long...
all kinds of substances that are used for the wrong,
a slight smell of dampness,
untidiness and dust,
unwashed clothes, plates and cups!

Fridge freezer - its empty and the water cold,
woodchip wallpaper, holes in the doors,
empty beer can's strewn over the floors!
A Betamax video, a black and white TV,
a picture of seagulls and a boat by the sea!

Draws full of letters,
final demands,
B.T., Littlewoods, the D.H.S.S.
all wanting money
or follow on address.

So what do you really think when I speak of my life?
What are your pictures of my house and home life?

Nothing At All

Why do you wish to cast a smile,
when it's not a smile at all,
why do you force tears from your eyes,
when you have no idea how to cry at all.

To pretend that you really love someone,
to make out you really care,
to hold my hand, to squeeze me tight,
to whisper in my ears.
To express to all that you would do,
louder than you have before,
To build a stage to reach out to all,
so they could see you from the stars.

To stand with me for all to see,
to parade what's really not there,
you masquerade and walk with me
with the hope that soon I'll fall,
and all the concern that comes our way...
is for you and not me at all.

You lie and deceive and mask your needs
and pretend that it's for me your there,
but you wish me to fail

leave devastation in my trail
so all the attention falls your way.

So the picture that is painted is of my blind hatred,
and it's you that suffered not me.
And the crocodile tears, and imaginary fears,
are truer reflection of what you've become.

To abandon me there, to leave to stare
along roads I don't wish to go.
But your heart of stone has left me alone,
you have got arms to fall,
and for all that you've gave me
in the years since a baby -
I'd rather have nothing at all.

Fresh Start

Your free to go now your time you have served,
no longer to suffer, no longer to hurt,
your liberty is returned now your life you can start.
"You're out of here, son, you can make a fresh start!"

We hope we have helped you to lead a promising life,
we hope we have taught you what's wrong and what's right
and when you're out there your happy and work hard,
we are sure you have the strength to make a fresh start.

So I'm no longer a number, a convict, a crook,
I'm no longer a liar, a varmint a nut!
The time I have spent here as wiped away all those things
It will be totally different with the life that it brings.

So I'm just like you are now, a prominent man,
full of excitement, ambition, and plans.
I won't have a problem, I'll live like you do,
all wants will come easy all dreams become true.

Your totally crazy! You don't have a clue!
Once I'm out there I'll be nothing like you...
nothing will come easy, few dreams will come true
...I'll be starting a new sentence to last my life through.

Maybe

Maybe I should leave this place,
take myself elsewhere.
Where would I go? Who would know?
What if I ended up nowhere?
Would I be missed, if I did this,
would anybody care out there?
I'd be on my own, all alone,
in this place, nowhere!

Maybe I should do it,
I know I want to do it,
but can I really do it,
am I brave enough to do it,
I'll just end up, nowhere!
It's the third time this week,
that I thought that I should do it,
but then I get so scared,
I'm really not prepared,
will I end up, nowhere!

No! Today I'm going do it,
I've thought so much of it.
But, I'm frightened.

No one will really miss me,
no one ever really talks of me,
but this time they will do,
more than they've ever had to,
and maybe, they'll miss me!

But my hands are shaking madly,
my heart is beating fast.
Is this knife sharp enough?
Do I really want to give this up?!

But no one will really miss me,
if I left this life completely,
they never come to see me,
except when they want to beat me!
I think I'll leave this life, completely!!

Broken

Carry me please - carry me,
as I'm too broken to walk anymore.
It's painful to take one more step -
too painful to take anymore.

I gave - you took, I cared to much,
your tears I cry for you.
I touch it burns - I feel your concerns,
I'll take your tears once again.

And though I am broken, weak with emotion
and every step is a cut that spills blood.
I'll have arms wide open though I am broken,
just to see that your smile is true.

And though I was broken you showed no emotion
and never helped to carry my load.
I would still walk with bleeding feet,
and touch you although it burns.

And if you were to stand there smiling,
I'd be happy though my blood spills.
And to carry you if I had to, though I am broken,
and your tears I'd cry again.

I would stand there besides you,
fight for you if I had too,
and take your pain
and carry it with mine.

I would do this for a lifetime,
take all your pain and tears,
and although I am broken I'd still want to know you.
Even though when I touch you it burns.

Sweet Maidens

I'd like to walk the ocean, and climb to touch the sun.
I'd like the world's hands to hold my hand,
and smile as we share what's good.
If the day it cries, our hands will wipe the tears,
we will make it smile, as we have smiled,
and use falling tears to feed the lands,
and the smiles that flow, will help what's needed grow.

And the moon will make a pact with the sun.
And the stars will shine much brighter,
and help lost sailors find their homes.
And the worry of their sweet maidens
will make good the soils that we tread.
And their children will grow and be happy,
and learn what ground they should tread.

And for those that have their own languages,
and need to share what we have to give.
We will give, as they have given to us,
their languages we should learn,
as our language they already know.
From action has no words were spoken,
that's why we cry today.

And this time will keep no secrets,
and no one or anything can carry a lie,
as the sea will become angry.
And the stars would not shine so bright,
and lost sailors will not find their way home.
And for those that have their own languages
would become fearful, and we could help no more.

So to hold each other, we must,
and to trust each other, is true,
so sweet maidens children will prosper,
and learn that the soil is rich.
And those that speak their own languages,
are friends with sea and the sun.
And the moon and the stars are sailors guides,
so sweet maidens can give us tomorrow.
And the sailors that made their way home,
had those with their own languages, as their companions.
And the stars, the sea, the sun and the moon
carried them home.

Will

Sometimes it's difficult,
really so tough,
feeling as low
as the dirt and the dust.

You feel so helpless, as though tied to the ground...
not able to move, no one hears your sounds.
You're tired of crying, your eyes they're sore...
you're tired of fighting your personal war.

You reach out hopefully, grasping at air...
only to realise there's no one there.
It hits you suddenly - like a gush of air...
you're all alone! Just you and despair.

But will is stronger than hurt and pain,
will is stronger than all your chains.
It's part of you, your souls compare
and nothing can hold you when will is there.

Karma

Why are people so hurtful, why are people so cruel?
What joy do they have, being so bad,
to the vulnerable that they choose?
To hurt somebody's feelings, to call them silly names,
to make them cry, even want to die,
to constantly cause them pain.

How can we be so heartless, so ruthless in attack?
To continue there, just standing there,
even knowing, they can't fight back.
To see little children crying, and older people too,
and just standing by watching them cry,
they're people like me and you.

Have you ever been a bully?!
Has bullying ever happened to you?
Have you stood there and laughed while you attack?
Or have you been on your knees,
begging saying "please...
no more from your attacks!"

Well if you've been a bully,
vicious - an arrogant twat.
There's a little thing called karma,

it watches everybody's back.

And what karma is,

it's the bullied kids way of fighting back.

It may not be tomorrow,

not even this time next week,

but it will come calling, without any warning...

and you will do more than weep!!

Jack's Visit

Autumn winds are blowing now,
leaves turn golden from green.
Some birds they leave for warmer tides,
others they come to play.

The sun that's born is younger now,
still younger when it leaves the day.
And the wind it carries needles,
as this days curtains come to close.

The earth's mirrors that we look upon,
tell us that they're cold.
And the swan it sits with its head amiss,
so strange for something so bold.

Jacks smoke it rides the lands wide,
marring all that breathes.
And his skin it paints all the land,
and the mirrors that don't rotate,
wear Jack's skin until young sun makes it smile.

Water spears hang menacing,
stopped in time - motionless,
until young sun lets them breath again.

As we walk upon Jack's skin,
he cracks his whip, until you feel your steps no more.
And bites your fingers and sends his needles in his breath
to pierce your ears.

Time is stopped - so it seems,
until crafty fox,
stops then trots,
and ravens sing a chorus with the crow.
Jack's visit is upon us, and soon there will be snow.
so kind of Jack to visit...
so kind to let us know.

Children

How much I miss them I really do,
the faces they pull, the things that they do.
My memory strays to the times that we've had,
most of them happy...some of them sad.

But what of them now? What will they do?
While I'm no longer there to say, "I love you".
Will they forget me like any stranger they see,
or am I still with them and always will be?

And what of the time when I'm sure to return?
Will it be wrong when they've still so much to learn?
But oh how I miss them, I really do!
I want to be there to say "I love you".

So please heavenly father far up above,
fill my children with all of my love.
Place them a picture deep in their minds...
of a father that loves them like no other kind.

Cold Love

Though a father I am - it is lost now.
Though kin walk with my blood
and conversation passes my ears,
"You're so much like your dad!"
To be present, but to not be,
to be close to touch, but too far away.
To see them so very closely,
though not to see - as if one's blind.
To wish conversation with thee,
though your creation, no common grounds.
To want hold so tight, with all your might,
but when the chance it accrues,
to close like a flower in the evening.

To know what to do as a father,
but have no idea what you're doing at all.
To speak words you know you should do,
but they really don't come from you!
To be there when they need you,
but feel you're a stranger
that's made of broken glass.
To want to say I love you,
but no words, will pass your lips.

To want show that you care,

and will always be there

but you come across as cold as snow.

These wishes that I've showed you

should not be wishes at all -

they're your god forsaken rite,

you should expect them outright

at no cost for pain or suffering.

But, all I can do, is apologise to you,

as on this way of life I have no bearing.

You see the bond that I need to help me succeed,

as the person that you should depend on...

was taken away on a terrible day -

as my love went away, my heart went astray

and my blood it ran cold, though young, I became old,

and that bond was snapped and taken.

To this very day most words that I say,

are not words that I wish spoken.

So when I do not reach out, please have no doubt,

it's not a choice that I am making.

I still love you the same,

but to me it's just a name

and I really don't know, how to give it.

So please if you could, my kin that I love,
understand it's a battle I'll keep fighting,
and although you don't see it
and it seems I don't give it.
It's there!
I just don't know, how to give it!

Empty

My guardian angel has left me - it seems I make her sad.
Her wings could not comfort me, her heart, I made feel bad.
My soul is not redeemable, its forgotten who I am,
I'm empty, it seems, empty as a shell,
or carcass that lies in the desert sun.
Even God could not clench my hands
- too cold for him to touch.

There was a time that I could love someone,
there was a time my touch could comfort,
and my arms could carry sadness,
and my strength would help move on.
Empty now, though a mannequin, I see nothing, cold.
Words I speak have no meaning, they do not touch a heart.

As the heart would stop and beat no more,
Cruel is what empty does,
to touch a sparrow it would fly no more,
To touch a bee it's flowers would turn black,
To stare at the sun it would burn no more.

The moon it sheds no light.
My life it had no choice it seems,
Empty is what I had to become,

No trust that I could offer,
And no trust would be offered to me.

Empty - to give is to take, and I gave all the time,
I miss my guardian angel, I hope she doesn't fall.
But to miss, is emotion, and emotion I have none,
And to think is to care, but care is also gone.

Empty. - to die does not fear me,
as I'm not allowed to die,
As my guardian angel has left me,
Along with my right to die - empty.

Snake's Garden

It's not happening 'ma', no words are the same,
my heads full of cartoons - I'm borderline sane!
Nothing makes sense no way to explain,
my minds full of rivers overflowing with pain.
The moon it's blood red,
the stars just like tears
and the wind - it is voices
stretching back from the years.

I hear babies - they're crying! Crying very loud
and there's pictures of faces upon every cloud.
Someone is calling me drawing me near...
then suddenly goes to later appear.
There are trees, trees, everywhere
all bearing fruits all ripe and rare!!..
The garden of Eden - but where is the snake?
Where is the temptation? The encouragement to take.

Fire, fire, fire that I see.
Where is this place? Where could I be?
And there in the fire, sits a large boat,
just calmly sat there staying afloat!
Lucifer, Lucifer the devil himself,

capturing souls to keep for himself.

Whispering, whispering - calling me home,
the voice of my mother, the voice of my own.
Come to me, come to me, that's no place to be!
No place for you and no place for me.
Awake, awake, I rise from my sleep,
very confused and wanting to weep!

I've been to the valley of life and death
and it's all up to you which way that you step,
many times I have been there at times that I sleep,
and every visions the same every path that I seek!
But something is missing for reasons not known
and I will leave it to you why the snake had not shown.

Answers

I go to bed, the nights they're lonely -
when I finally sleep,
the night its old,
and when the sun smiles
upon my face in the mornings -
a river of tears have flowed.

I ask myself questions, no answers I find,
for the long lonely nights,
and the tears I've cried,
it's hurtful and painful,
and it's hard though I've tried,
to find no end to the start of these times.

I become lost in my motion, lost in my own mind,
frustrated and angry,
no answers I find,
I toss and I turn,
stand up and sit down,
go round in circles, round and round.

My fists become clenched,
my eyes they see red,
I'm afraid every night to go to my bed,

its answers I seek,

its answers I want,

they're all that is needed for me to move on.

For years I've been searching,

and wanting to know,

for the long lonely nights,

and the tears that I flow,

But, it's obvious now to me that I think,

for the answers I need, the answers I seek.

I do not have them, they won't come from me,

there's others that have them,

others not me,

So I will just wait here, patiently, still,

with the hope that these others

will bring my answers...they will!

Fate

Do you sit where we used to sit?
And gently hold my hand?
Do you walk where we used to walk?
And think of our wonderful plans?
Do you dance where we used to dance -
among the forests trees?
Do you collapse to the floor -
where we used to before?
In our loving grasp.

Do you smile and giggle, skip and whistle -
Along the wooded path?
Do you run and hide, I'd count to five,
Before wanting smell would give you away?
Do you miss all of this?
Do you miss me to kiss?
Do you wish it as much as I do?

Is there word's that should be spoken,
although we are broken -
to reach out to each other no more?
Would you change anything?
Do anything?

So what's broken could now be fixed,

or is our time over?

To be - no longer?

Or do you linger to what you know is not there?

Do you fall to your knees?

Ask God and plead,

to make all that hurts go away?

Lost Sons

Don't cry any more, dry your eyes,
the pain and the tears they will all subside,
we'll stand here beside you every step of the way!
A shoulder to cry on, an ear when you speak,
we'll no longer leave you - that's a promise to keep.

The pain deep inside, you the tears that you weep,
the anger frustrations, the daily taunt of your grief!
Be strong my friend, use my strength as your own,
you will no longer suffer or walk this alone.

I cannot replace these sons you have lost...
I can't take their place like the snow after frost.
But if the Lord would allow it
and no pain would foresee...
I would gladly exchange your lost one for me.

Shallow Dreams

Shallow dreams,
we wish for things -
though shallow they may be.
You dream, I dream,
we all have dreams -
you, them and me.

Without our dreams,
though like shallow streams -
they make us who we are.
To have no dreams,
what would it mean?
Would it change that what we are?

Without our dreams,
we're empty beings -
and dull and grey we are.
No stories to share,
with those who care
and smile as we share them.

It's nice to dream,
of different scenes
and to feel happiness for a while.

To be somewhere nice,

with someone you like -

it's what dreams are made for.

I want all to dream,

but of happy scenes -

so there's happiness we can hold on to.

As life can be cruel,

so terribly cruel -

and our dreams are there for this reason.

To keep our minds sane

and on a level plain -

so the turmoil of life we can conquer.

So enjoy your shallow dreams,

hang on to what they mean -

they're for you and your life's next chapter!

Tears

Buried is my past - buried deep,
but not to lose all of it, some of it I must keep.
So to allow for me to understand,
And to allow others to understand me,
But much of it must be buried,
Much of it really deep,
But it does not really leave me,
It's just hidden deep within,
To appear when I'm most vulnerable,
To appear when I'm most weak,
But many masks I have to hide this,
Many words I can speak,
At these times that I'm most vulnerable,
At the times that I'm most weak,
It's painful to make a tear fall,
As my life it needs to cry,
But to cry I become weaker still,
As I've allowed these tears to fall,
But I don't understand the tear,
I cannot see which ones are true,
Do I need to feel the beats of someone's heart,
Or the words that someone speaks,
Do I need to touch and feel them,

And the tears, then they will speak,
I feel nothing for these tears,
They are not friends of mine,
Tears to me are liars,
and a million lies the tears have told,
Whether you're just a child,
Or whether your someone old.
Liars. I choose to have no tears,
So if to lie, would have to speak,
But others I think will keep their tears,
So to hurt the vulnerable and the weak,
Then go and laugh and praise themselves,
As they pretend to weep.

Cosmic Mate

A penny for your thoughts,
a wish full of dreams.
Solemn are we, lonely,
with this life that we lead.

Memories of happiness,
many tears for one's shame,
tenderness, comfort, the magic of your touch,
my cosmic mate who I love so much.

Thoughts that I have
which cause me much pain
of times I have hurt you
and caused you much shame.

I am one of hatred
and deserve much less!
You should cast me aside
and leave me to fest

.

Why do you offer so much love from your soul?
Why does it grow stronger as we grow old?
To you I'm a stranger. I change like the wind!
What is your secret? What joy do I bring?

I should be down on my knees -
begging at your feet,
for all your forgiveness,
with each word that I speak!

But you my love...
my cosmic mate
want nothing from me...
despite my hate.

On The Canvas

Why is my life so difficult?
Why am I such a twat?
Why do I screw up everything I love,
with no consequence of what will come back?
What do I do wrong?
I try to be strong -
but strong ends up a disaster!
I try to do right and what's wrong I will fight.
But, I'm the one on the canvas!

Am I really so screwed up -
that I should be locked up?
My life it shows no purpose...
yet, I feel and I cry
and sometimes I wish to die.
Work for no money -
to help those that are suffering.
Yet, I still end up on the canvas!

I try to do what's good,
and do what I should,
to make my passage in this life righteous.
But, I always screw up!

Make my life so tough
and end up back on the canvas!

Do I drink too much?
Do I talk too much?
Am I, just too much?!
I wish I could find some answers.
But the chances are...I won't.
And I will end up on the canvas!

Wish

I couldn't wish for anymore,
than lying next to you,
To have you here, so close and near,
So close to touch your skin.

To kiss your lips, when I wish,
to look deep inside your eyes,
To stroke your hair, to feel your there,
your breath sends shudders down my skin,

And every time, our skins they bind,
excites me from deep within.
To hold each other tightly, our bodies they are one,
And there's not a place that I could wish, to be with anyone.

To lie and see you sleeping,
is a privilege that I have,
and there's not a soul, however bold,
would have the strength to move me on.

I'd stay there for my lifetime,
and read you stories when you sleep,
and when you rise, open up your eyes,
another vision that I will keep.

And I'll wish for more, a whole lot more,
   of these times our bodies meet,
So to have you close, so very close,
   when again our skins they meet.

So when the time it comes, that we may not hold,
   there's enough that's buried deep within,
So to keep us going, both us knowing,
   All we have to do is wish.

The Jester

Obviously disruptive, disrespectful and a fool,
self-centred and obsessive.
Gratitude is non-existent, politeness just a myth,
no time for advice - just a stiff upper lip.
There's a chip on my shoulder
which is like a mountain to oneself...
it is yet to be conquered, climbed and explored.
It is yet to mapped out - all its regions ignored.
There's a valley in my mountain,
a sanctuary of my own!
A place of solitude anger and pain,
a place of self-abuse, grievance and shame.
All outsiders are intruders, full arrogance and poor values,
yet they try to explore- searching for answers....
without questions before.
Personalities are ruptured,
leaning to more or less,
searching for reasons for reasons why
as the whole thing excites them like orgasm to their minds.
Yet who is the fool here?
The jester to see!
Have you found any answers?
This persons just me!

Voices

Imaginary friends with voices,

crowding and twisting my head.

Always there,

forever there.

Why won't they leave my head?!

They say they're friends,

my only friends.

To trust them,

we know best.

But, the things they say

- every day, all day.

It's just not right, it can't be right!

But is it right!

They say it's right...the voices!

We're your friends,

your only friends.

Do as we say, not as we do,

listen to, the voices!

But you're not there,

there's no one there!

But if we're not there and there's no one there...

then whose are the voices?!
There's something wrong,
something very wrong,
this can't be right, it's got to be wrong.
I need to fight you, I really need to.
The voices!

When I sleep at night, every night,
you still appear - make out you're here.
You tell me things, many things,
I wish you to go, I need you to go...
I thought we weren't here -
there was nobody here.
Imaginary friends, that's what is here,
so very near, we are here!
The voices!

Remember Me

Remember me will you, remember for who I was,
Remember that was true about me,
and also that not so good.
When you talk of me, be not afraid to curse,
speak of my misgiving, be not afraid to hurt.

But also talk kindly, if you seen I had a heart,
So to smile when you talk of me,
and what happiness did I bring,
But also feel a little sad for me, but try to forgive if you can.
When you think of me, think kindly,
as I'd think kindly of you.

But do not forget the hurt I caused,
As I know there's hurt I caused you.
When I come to you in your dreams,
Do not wake from your sleep,
for I come to you for a reason,
There will be words I need to speak,
But to know and remember me, as I truly was.

For I cannot take this journey, if all that's said is good,
I will not be allowed to bring happiness, care, and love,
You need to remember me truly,

with all that's bad and good,
So if allowed to return again,
and in whatever life I come.

A clear and crystal path I leave,
and a conscience clear of what I've done,
But you will have to remember, all the sins that I have done,
As all bridges I have burnt myself,
forgiveness will not come.

God cannot forgive me, He does not listen to what I say,
So you must now ask for my forgiveness,
As you are pure and true,
And you remember who I was,
good and bad it's true,
And he will see your kindness,
your strength, your love,
And that you remembered me for my badness,
alongside the good.

Everywhere

A gentle breeze

upon my face,

a pleasant thought, your warm embrace.

A singing bird

upon my ears,

your gentle words from all our years.

The warmth of sun

upon my skin,

your tender touch from love within.

The scent of flowers,

their pretty looks...

you're all around - I feel your touch.

You will always be with me,

right here by my side,

I won't let you go you keep me alive!

I think of these comforts,

I look upon them each day

and you'll always be with me every step of the way.

Minds Existence

To be graceful in my elegance,
to masquerade my own desires,
to balance and switch my minds existence,
to juggle my life,
and all of its strife,
I feel there's something missing,
that I should be giving,
to find it's a matter of principles.

I give twisted expressions,
look up to the heavens!
There's a fire in my soul,
raging out of control.
I'm angry! I'm mad!
Want to scream out and shout!
There's misgivings that I'm seeing,
they hamper my minds existence.

I'm going to ride chariots of fire,
through my minds deep desires,
to climb mountains of the past,
where I've stumbled and cracked,
to a place where I shouldn't be going.

Where my sanity rides a white horse,
it's lassoing my thoughts.
It chokes their very existence!

To be released and set free,
they're prisoners to my own stability.
Swim through the seas of my mind,
where there's planted seeds I don't find,
yet they exist in my minds existence'
To harvest what's grown from these seeds of the unknown,
to muster all strength in my own defence,
and ride hard, with my chariots of fire!

To bring down the white horse,
that my sanity's aboard,
so to comfort my minds existence.
There's no cards to be played
for its anger and rage
and it bleeds of sheer hate
and draws swords for debate,
to swallow what it can, what's left of this man.
And destroy my minds own existence!

Distant Lands

To sail the seas a wish I have,
to venture far and wide,
many a place I'd love to see -
with only the stars as my guide.

To land wherever the winds will take,
to cast ashore some ancient lands,
to be not afraid of where I am,
fearful of no foreign lands.

To drop anchor where the seasons land,
to embrace what there is to find,
to make fire and camp, and light a lamp,
so others they may find.

To feast upon this lands riches,
make use of all I'd find.
To gaze at the stars at night,
to paint pictures on every cloud.

To send my stories far and wide,
carried by the seas,
this place I would stay awhile,
until fair winds called my name.

Then off again, to do the same,
sail to distant lands,
to find culture I know not of,
and share culture of my own.

A legacy, a prophecy,
with arms open wide,
to sail again, again, again,
until my ship can sail, no more.

Then a new adventure I will take,
whether land, seas or more,
to go with it, to flow with it,
I'd want more, more, more.

And at a time, my body, it can take no more,
and wherever I may be,
I'll take my passing smiling,
there will be no regrets from me.

As I have travelled to distant lands,
a wish that I fulfilled,
with my only friends.
My loyal friends - the oceans.

Golden Waters

Natures breath warms my face, while God's creatures
gracefully place...melodies upon my ears,
colours of plenty dance across my path...
as though calling me to them to reveal secrets of the past.
Touching them, feeling them, fills my soul with desire.

A passion for living, a passion for love,
a desire to believe in all that's good.
High above me, amongst the pictures in the sky,
having graced their stories to many a mankind,
to reveal what I wish, what my mind chooses to take,
then to wander through lands riches to a place
where sanity of mind is all but a distance away.

Then to walk on golden waters feel God's air -
like silk upon my skin,
and love in my veins and a passion so intense
with the power to touch the stars,
and keep it forever in the depths of my mind,
so to travel there again to hold it, to touch it,
to keep it forever at a time I choose,
at a time that's mine.

Moments

For every moment I'm not with you,
is a moment I have lost.
It's moments that will never come back,
these moments I have lost.
I long for you to be here with me, every single day
and though you're not that far from me,
I still miss you anyway.

My heart knows that you're not around,
it whimpers deep within my chest,
it slowly calls out your name,
as it knows it's friend is missed.

To sit, or walk, or even talk,
brings happiness deep within.
These moments that I share with you,
is the reason, my heart you win.
And I hope our journey it never ends,
and forever more we're side by side,
for if these moments were ever to disappear,
I'd truly think, I'd died.

Kiss

For all we see,
touch and hold,
a gentle feeling,
a comfort,
a meaning,
a reason for strength,
a purpose for living,

An ambition to keep
what's whole and honest.
A bond so solid,
impossible to break,
A time we remember,
to never forget,
A time that is ours,
always forever.

The time of the kiss.

Hearts Cannot Be Shared

Just a little twinge...that's all it was...
not as bad as I thought it would be.
No tears at all fell that day...
and little sadness came to me.

It seems my thoughts in times that past
were an armour to my heart
and all the hurt that came my way
was stopped and made to part.

I feel my life will change now
like a snake that sheds its skin,
and all the doubts I had before
lost so deep within.

Though I still may think and cast a smile
of times we dearly cared.
The time has come to understand
ones heart cannot be shared.

Expectations

Broken promises, from distant times,
that leave wounds hard to heal,
painful still today,
though born for many years.
The shaking of my hands
and trembling lips,
the heart-wrenching pulling,
still today, as years apart!
Weakness exposed, out in the cold,
no comfort from feeling,
emotions left reeling,
to die every time my eyes shed sad reason.
To expect now what's there,
all the years -
no repair,
it's to rape my whole reason for living.
So to break out with expression,
to show strength and compassion,
use pain as the way to become ruthless!
So because of the years of torment and tears,
and no signs of the healings coming
and the forever running,
as this is all I've learnt to master.

So expectations were once high,
but then to realise their lies
and for those that factor,
could bring an end to this matter,
were weak, and now become weaker!
But to me it's no joke!
For the false promises they spoke,
and no reasons they give,
for all the years of my grief
and still no answers for my expectations.
So it's with beaten emotions
and heart stopping notions,
and my now, selfish motions,
that I stand before you today!
And to want for so long,
though not in the wrong,
was a hurtful and painful existence,
so my saga now ends
without happy end...
was it too much for my expectations!

Your Song

May I sing a song for you,
That sends secrets to your ears,
May there also be some whispers there,
That make you fall happy tears,
May my chorus make your heart beat fast,
And send shivers down your spine,
May my words make you think to yourself,
This song is really mine.

Will you take every word I sing,
And hold them tightly in your hands,
Will you keep them there, forever there,
So to listen to them when you choose,
Or to share them with someone close,

As my words maybe they could use.
Will you keep them with you always,
And listen every day.

Will they make you smile, for a little while,
Will they help you through your day,
Will you sing them when the day is old,
And your body takes retreat,
Will they carry you, through the night,

Will you let them join your dreams?
And when the sun, brings warmth upon,
Will you listen once again?
Will you smile, as the day is long,
share laughter with your friends,

And when your home, all alone,
Will you listen once again,
Would you dance along, to your song
As my whispers make you smile,
And for a while, just a little while,
Could you kiss the words I sing,
So when the chorus flows,
And that your song it knows,
it's yours and yours to keep.

Joyful Amazing Kind Everlasting

They say you are a lucky boy
to have a mum like me
but to you my friend I tell you this...
the lucky one is me.

You are my life - I live for you,
there is nothing that I want more
and if you ever asked me to
I'd walk to every shore.

We all have dreams and pleasant thoughts
of what our lives should be,
but to just have you here by my side
is good enough for me.

I love you son, I love you lots
and I will love you more each day,
and if it was that you were not
my life would be so grey.

But the Lord has graced me with your presence
and for that I thank and pray,
and you'll always be my special friend
until my final day.

Running

To be ripped and abused,
tormented and used,
to be beaten and hit for somebody's kicks.
To be left on the floor,
crying and unsure,
to reach out for their love -
when its them with the gloves!
To cry yourself to sleep,
which you'll do for many weeks.
To be beaten half to death,
but you still hunger their respect!
To clean blood up all the time,
tell your friends "It's not mine"!
To lie to yourself,
believe what comes out their mouths -
"It won't happen again",
but you know that's just lame!
They won't let it go...
it's all that they know
and you are the one that will be screaming!
So to not waste your love,
for more bruises and blood -
your power will come from your footsteps!

And though it will be hard,

and tear at your heart,

and you will feel sorry,

for the one that hurts your body.

And tears you will cry,

despite all the lies...

but it's for your footsteps you should be listening.

Because as the story goes,

as you already know...

...there's no running, before you are walking!

Special Someone

I know a special someone,
so very special you'll see.
They're always there to show they care,
especially for me.
When I'm in the doldrums,
and feeling very sad,
and don't know where to turn to,
and my day's been very bad.

That certain special someone,
appears there by my side,
to lift me up, to kick my butt,
to tell me to get a grip.
It doesn't matter where I am,
or even what the time,
they're always there to carry me,
and catch me when I fall.

And at times when I'm difficult,
an idiot, a spoilt brat -
that very special someone remains
although I am a prat.
At times when I'm foolish,

show no respect for cash,
and leave myself on my arse,
guess who's there to catch.

I owe this special someone,
more than I could possibly give,
and if not there to show they cared,
not sure how I would live.
So to this special someone,
that does so much for me,
I solemnly swear, for all your care,
and this life you've helped me keep.

That I will thank you daily,
and all promises I will keep,
and every night, if you like,
do that stuff you like with your feet!

What Place?

Imagine a place, a place of your own,
a place you visit, just you alone.

Would yours have a heaven? A god? A hell?
Would it have children, fields and trees?
Would it have riches for you to please?
Would there be hunger? Famine and war?
Would there be rivers that flow no more?

Would there be poverty, corruption and lies?
Would there be horrors not meant for your eyes?
Would there be people full of hate,
full of resentment, in your place?
Would there be violence, racism, and crime?

Would there be too much...too much for your mind?
Would there be sadness, heartbreak and death?
Would there be worry in every gasp of your breath?
Would the night bring fear, nightmares and ghosts?
Would sleep be impossible? No laughter, no jokes.

Imagine a place a place of your own,
a place you visit - just you alone.

Shoes

For heavy burden I carry on my shoulders,
for distant truths that were really lies.
To walk on as I do today,
to be able to look in people's eyes.

I am but just a normal soul,
God's love I feel in my heart...
...yet it is a lonely walk through life I take,
and I feel so much I need to give.

But, to give,
I see my own desire,
that I should be looked upon as good,
because I want to give.

Is this not a purpose for who I am,
or do I search and long,
to be someone else,
yet it is my path I walk along,

I will take what is offered,
yet feel I am not offered enough,
am I wrong to continue to walk this path!
Or am I wearing someone else's shoes!

Is it then, that I am not who I am?
And have stolen treasures that were not meant for me,
and I should burn at the end of this path I walk,
as the shoes I wear, are not meant for me!

Done More

I can't believe these feelings,
that's tearing at my heart,
I can't believe these emotions,
that's ripping me apart.
I close my eyes to see you,
reach out to try to touch,
I try to bring you closer to me,
the one I love so much.

Then the truth it finally hits me,
the reality and the facts,
that these are just my memories,
it's a life that's in the past.
As I walk along the riverbank,
and through these fields of green,
I close my eyes and think of you,
but find the pain is just a dream.

When I sit there and I'm lonely,
and the tears begin to fall,
I find myself asking my soul,
is it time to end it all.
When I rise from another empty night,

and call out to no one there,

my heart it sinks a thousand ships,

I wish that you were there.

When I see the laughing children,

the birds up in the air,

and every cloud that I see,

is a picture of you just there.

It's hard to carry on this life,

I miss your helping hand,

and all the love I had to give,

is now scattered across the lands.

So the truth is, our time is over,

it's a path we take no more,

and I will just grow older,

with the wish that I'd done more.

Truth Or Lies

Wealth and fortune,
poverty and disease.
Promises broken,
secrets told.
Broken hearts, people get old.

Children taken, women raped,
terrorist bombs, earthquakes,
tidal waves, guerrilla wars.
Hurricanes, tornados, lightning strikes
there's no mail tomorrow the posts on strike.

Murder, torture, perverted abuse.
Child pornography, ritual abuse.
Social unrest - another broken truce.
Factories closing, no hospital beds.
You can't go to school the teachers have said.

Banks they're closing -
your pension's worth shit.
You can't get a job
they've closed all the pits.

Children grow hungry,
the old they get cold
and you've got capitalist pigs
on your centre fold.

Labour's done nothing, the Lib-Dem's are just wimps
and the Tories just want to make you jump of a bridge.
So let's go and smash a window, maybe steal a car!
Start a revolution or have we gone too far?!

Militants are everywhere, neo-Nazis too.
All living there together -
with some immigrants near Crewe!
Claiming social housing, queuing at the DHSS
claiming for everything.....this country's a mess!

Willow Tree

I watch from the shadows of the willow tree,
her beauty steals my breath.
Bare footed, she dances amongst the daffodils,
and in turn, they dance with her.
She smiles and laughs, and as a chat,
to whoever she believes is there.
Her beautiful long dress, her auburn hair,
no match, for what graces my eyes.

Her beauty so much that it's dangerous,
many a man would fall in her wake,
her eyes would pierce the darkest night,
let alone pierce a heart.
Her hair, a gentle dance parades,
as she turns to kiss the sun.
Her skin, I touch, though far away,
and bring my fingers to my lips.

Her scent for something so beautiful,
Must be magical, to belong to her,
no flower on earth, would bring it justice,
as pure, is what is there,
Her body it move's, so elegantly,

and all nature moves elegantly with her,

they follow her command,

as they understand,

it's their desire, to wish to do so.

As the evening,

it moves in closer,

her silhouette,

comes closer to me,

to reach out and touch,

but not that much,

to break cover,

from the shadows of the willow tree.

Jollies

If I were to go on my jollies, these are who I'd take,
Jack and Jill they would be brill, we'd only need a spade.
Mr Grumpy, Humpty Dumpty,
if we could get him off Grumpy's wall!
Jack and his beanstalk with that chick with the golden eggs!
So money to spend, but that depends,
if his giant friend's still in bed.

The Grand Old Duke of York, and ten thousand of his men.
In case that Jack dude's giant friend,
decides to get out of bed!
Snow White and her seven companions,
as they could share a room,
and me and Snow White could hang around
and have lazy afternoons.

The Owl and the Pussycat, as they can sail a boat,
and the cow and it's spoons -
along with the moon,
so we could see at night,
The Princess and her pea, as she's got lots of beds,
for the Duke of York's ten thousand men
have somewhere to lay their heads.

Cinderella and her pumpkin, and her four mischievous mice,
because if we're stuck, before midnight struck,
her chariots will suffice!
Goldilocks and her three bears, they have got to come,
as they've got lots of porridge, for everybody's tum,
and goldilocks don't give a toss, any cot, she will stop!

Little Red Riding Hood, she could be a laugh,
and she's got that wooden basket,
with food in there she's stashed!
A handsome prince, we need a prince,
For the princess she might fall ill,
and just one kiss from the princes lips, is like a magic pill!

But where to go, you want to know,
a difficult choice to make,
Neverland is boring, and its cold this time of year,
The Lost World's lost its character,
and all its animals now roam free -
last year I took seven dwarfs but ended up with three!

I want to go somewhere lovely,
somewhere really nice,
I'll invite Captain Pugwash,
and let him lead our plight,

when I've asked him in the past,
it's usually good advice.

I'll take you all, it's not a haul,
its somewhere really nice,
with rolling seas and lots of trees,
and the weather is calm and still,
we'll have some fun and laughter,
with my mate Portland Bill!

Barriers

Contemplating the future,
reminiscing from the past.
Trying to find the answers...
from questions long since asked.

Memories come to haunt me,
as many as there are stars.
Bringing emotional torture
and opening ancient scars.

The pain that's deep within me
runs through my veins like blood
submerging every part of me
and drowning all my love.

I feel so tired and helpless,
like a soul whose time has passed,
the strength I once had with me
has gone like seasons past.

All the steps I take are painful...
though as walking on broken glass.
All the air I breath is poison...
like a batch of harmful gas.

I need to break these barriers
to free the pain within,
I need to open up my dreams
and let some goodness in.

Smiles

For faith of giving, I send a smile,
to fly like birds across the lands.
To land upon all those that wish them,
and let them smile too
and who to give them.

To bring happiness to all, to smile in our own world's,
to find comfort and meaning,
for what we are giving.

May our smiles cover the oceans,
and to reach those that are lost and lonesome,
so, they too can smile and be happy,

You see our smiles they are free,
and happy people will be,
just for the sake of your giving.

And as time does go by,
your smile will never die,
and these people that you've smiled,
it will be buried in their minds...

...and they too, will walk on smiling.

Weaker

If I was to walk a lonely road, would you walk with me?
If I became weak, so very weak, would you help,
to show that you care and need me,
Or would you become scared,
as you're not prepared,
to accept that I can become weaker.

Though I'm so strong, to carry you along.
If I'm weak, you become heavier,
And for all that I want to, sometimes I cannot do,
what's expected as I'm so weak.
But although I'm weaker, and will become weaker,
what strength I have is yours,
and will bleed from my knees, to please you,

As you need me to be stronger.
As you no longer,
have faith that I will carry you along.
And as much as I want to, and try so much too,
I am, but simply a man and my heart can be broken,
And words that are spoken, can break me,
And make me fall to my knees!

If you really love me and want me and need me,

though weaker, you'll still hold my hand.
And as I do carry you, because that's what I want to,
You're lighter as your holding my hand.
I'm here because I want to, need you and love you.
And life without you has no plans,

But though I'm stronger
and want you longer,
it's you that makes me carry this load!
And although my tears will fall longer
and I become weaker,
I will still carry your load!

Because without you there's nothing,
my life would be suffering,
So strong! I have nothing to give.
But the time it is coming,
that you might come running,
that I have given you everything I could give.

Really Love You

So long it has been now,
many months they have passed.
Many seasons we've seen,
many bridges we've crossed.
Many tears we have shed,
many times we have laughed.
Many times we have parted
only then to come back.

The pain I have caused you,
the suffering the hurt.
The lies I have told you...
I'm as low as the dirt.
Your heart is a mountain,
your faith it is too.
And although I have problems
I really love you.

I'll always be grateful,
forever in your debt.
Through times that are difficult
and when all seems so hard
I'll be right here besides you

I'll give you my heart.
I know I've been selfish,
and at times untrue,
but although I have problems,
I really love you.

Wings Of Gold

I whisper gently in your ear,
of how much you mean to me.
To thank you for the many years,
of the happiness you've brought to me.

I know there's times, in these times,
difficult I could be,
and have bought you tears through the years,
with the problem, that is me.

But, strong you are, and brave you've been,
for, it's not easy, what comes with me,
and many have tried, but to fall by the side,
or to leave with uncertainty.

I have seen you struggle, I've made you cry,
I've bought you trouble, I've told you lies,
yet, here you still remain, a mountain of strength,
all for my defence, I thank god, your by my side.

And still to this day, though still a distance away,
the time, my life will bring happier times,
you still remain, despite there's still pain,
that you will suffer, for your protection of me.

So, to you this my love,

I pray to above,

that you should be given wings of gold,

for all that you've given.

Suffered and listened,

cried and supported,

carried and sorted,

this complex and distorted, difficult life...that's me.

Stronger

Come into my arms and rest awhile,
close your eyes and drift where you wish,
remain in this place between sleep and life,
feel its power, its elegance its grace,
feel safe here, not fearful, feel wanted,
not disposed, feel found, not lost.

This place is yours, it belongs to you,
and while you're here, no harm to you,
and at times when your sad, as we often become,
my arms will become stronger, and so will you,
and as we become stronger, and stronger still,
our love will become more powerful for me - for you.

And we together, will move as one,
we will face all obstacles that venture our way,
We will battle all battles that stand in our way,
Our strength shall be glorious, our power immense,
We shall become giants and crush all our doubts.
Stronger now, that's what we are,
stronger now, than ever before.

Because although I hold you, in my arms you sleep,
and because of our love, oh so deep,

without you I'd be nothing, and so very weak,
you are the one with the strength that I speak,
you are the one that keeps us complete,
and although I have wished you here, into my arms,
you are the stronger, and it's your arms, I seek.

Solvent Dreams

Such a feeling of self-being,
a sense of security within my world,
a dome surrounds me from all that hurts.

A private place for me and my thoughts.
I'm protected here, what comes I bring,
dreams of happiness smiles and joy,
all that's within my personal toys.

I bring the elfins, the fairy, the ghosts,
I bring the stories that I wrote:
a hermits kingdom, a sanctuary of my own...
I have nothing to fear once within my dome.

Down

To grasp at feelings from deep within,
to call out, to no one listening,
to reach out to no one there,
to clutch at straws,
to punch the walls -
this is how I'm feeling.

To feel desperate for someone's caring,
to want to fall deep into someone's arms,
to cry alone, all alone,
to feel that nobody as a heart.
To feel desperate and isolated,
lost with no hope of being found.

To scream and shout, the need to break out,
for the sake of your own sanity.
To realise all this you have to battle alone,
for the placebo does not make it go away,
to understand, that where you stand,
is alone, every step of the way.

They say they're here to help you,
take your hand, and guide your way,
but, that's all they can do,

is to talk like this to you,
as your madness,
they have no control.

For years it's been growing like a tumour,
deep within your head,
just waiting for that reason,
that excuse, to make you fall apart.

And now your madness it has no boundaries,
it does not care, for what stands in its way,
it will rip you apart, push loved ones afar,
and leave you standing there, shivering.

And you will feel lonely, desperate, angry and lost,
and your loved ones and friends,
can only pretend,
they understand what it is that you've got.

Lost

Submerged,
I feel trapped,
lost in a place,
with no getting back.
No one to turn to,
no one to see,
no one at all,
except only me.

How did I get here?
This choice was not mine!
There must be a reason;
some answers to find.
I go round in circles,
it's so hard to think;
I must have a purpose;
surely you'd think.

But for years I've been here,
submerged, trapped,
and for years I've been trying
to find my way back.
I've asked for forgiveness,

so many times,
so I could move on -
leave all this behind.

I try to help others,
I try to be kind,
I try to share my experience,
so others survive.
So this is my purpose,
why I've remained lost,
feeling submerged,
many years for this cost.

I was meant to suffer: so others will not,
to prevent them from drowning,
becoming so lost,
See we all have a purpose,
fate, and a path,
a reason for living, to give something back.

Mine it was painful,
difficult and to last,
But now I'm happy,
glad of my path,
so I could help others,
to find their way back.

Bang Shout Bang

Awakened by banging, raised voices downstairs,
quieter for a moment....then louder than before,
sobbing from my mother, mumbled words I can't make out,
then it gets louder switching verbal attacks.

Chairs get broken, pictures get smashed,
doors they get slammed more verbal attacks.
My sisters awake now, my brother is too....
frightened to death wondering what they can do!

So I wander downstairs - to do what, I don't know!
Just hoping when they see me....all the noises will go!
When I finally get there - he has my mom by the hair...
I call him a 'bastard' but he just gives me a stare.

My mum she is shaking, crying with fear!
I wonder what she thinks - just seeing me here?
My dad's gone to bed now - the shouting as stopped,
my mom will sleep downstairs, unusual it's not.

For days there is friction,
we are all scared to breathe.
I just sit in my bedroom, to keep out the way...
my mum and my dad still have nothing to say.

Shackles

Greater steps I try to make,
but seemed shackled to the ground,
my stride is long, but goes nowhere,
I seem to be left behind.

I strive for positivity,
to achieve what I want to achieve,
to never give up no matter how tough,
although you try to keep me shackled.

My life from the past, is positive at last,
and I will break away from these shackles,
as there are people I see, that are needy of me,
and your shackles will not prevent me from giving.

I will use all my might, and help them to fight,
your giving of these shackles,
Because as you can see, there people like me,
and you will be held accountable for your shackles.

See, all that you fear, is what you put here
and your solution and cure it is shackles,
but over the years, I faced up to these fears
and your shackles they snap like cotton!

And I will do all in my power,
keep going and endeavour,
so those shackled
will be shackled no longer!

And they will move on, on and on,
and become stronger in their process...
...and they will achieve, and you will concede,
your shackles were never the answer!

Think

To be happy is a must I think,
but so is to be sad,
Because, if were never sad,
how do we know what's bad,
It's best to regret something you have done,
than something that you've not,
As if you've no regret, then cold, are we not!

No emotion you could give someone
And no emotion you'll receive,
A cold and lonely figure, alone, with no one near,
Alone is not pleasantry, when no one sees your tears,
and alone is always a very long time,
it can seem like many years,
There's no love that you can offer
and no love will come to you,
As you're a lonely figure, there's no one there but you.

So to cry you'd have no comfort, no one to wipe your tears,
no one to hold you tight, alone, to face your fears.
To grow and learn is normal, to hurt and cry the same,
but you as a lonely figure, who's to share your pain?
So a lonely figure we shouldn't be,

a lonely figure that's lost,
and emotion and pain is what we should gain,
to prevent us from being lost,
as we can always feel our pain,
but, for others to see is a must,
as without this we are lonely, confused and very lost.

So to take the pain and fear the same,
it's got to be a must,
as a sad and lonely figure, stands alone,
and cry's so very much.
So hurt we must allow to come,
we all must feel some pain,
as without the pain and suffering,
we would all become the same.

Autumn Leaves

Autumn leaves fall gracefully to the ground
having blessed us with their short lives.
Trees become naked,
shedding their skins,
sleeping now, until called upon again.

To please our eyes with a multitude of colours
and a sound so pleasant,
that babies sleep long and content,
listening to their stories,
a different one for every tree.

Growing now from pod to flower,
inviting birds of plenty to sing with the leaves,
to reside there - a life that creates life,
and make their worlds once again.
A gift a joy for all to share.

Cold Blood

For strength of conscious
and whispers that are lies,
to walk your road with head held high -
when all you do is lie.

To cut away, and take a soul,
and enjoy the taste of blood.
Your hands they're dirty...
they will not come clean!

Your lies are hot they burn,
you have no emotions for the pain you cause,
you walk through life, with no hint of shame...
you do not deserve a name!

You walk in and leave suffering,
your black heart, it pumps cold blood,
you have no idea of giving love...
as no love has come to you.

I pity you - I really do,
but, still a chance of my heart I would still give,
though cold blood it runs through your heart,
I still would like to give!

For cruel your passage it has been,
and blame is a heavy burden to haul...
though, you take no blame - at all!

But you must search your soul within
and question what your heart desires.
Look so deep within,
for cold blood it leads your path for you
and every day, another sin!

So with haste, take these words I give,
and take the hand, I offer to you,
so blame, it now is lighter,
and cold blood, will slowly warm...
...and you will feel love at last,
and your name, be gladly called.

Helentree

How I love to be here,
Lying next to you.
To see your eyes, to smell your hair,
To kiss your lips, to hold you bare.
Your tiny nose, your sticky out ear,
Your old woman's knees,
Your wee small feet, your little toes I love to eat,
Your hands I hold, your fingers too,
the way they spell, I love you,
The way we frog, the way we spoon,
The way you sleep until afternoons.
The way you snore, your teeth you grind,
You've got the very best behind.
Your leg so long to wrap around me,
They squeeze the very life from me.
The books you read, the way you cook,
The way you tell Fred, "that's enough"!
The way you walk down the street,
With your very bouncy feet.
The only one to keep up with me,
The only one you've got to be,
The way we chat, the way we laugh,
The way you move that lovely ass.

First Night

Lost and alone in my minds despair,
clinging to memories that I know, were once there.
Searching deep and deeper still,
burrowing and burrowing further still,
searching, hoping, pleading that I will find
answers, reasons, facts,
feeling the urge to scream out loud,
feeling the urge to fight what hurts.

Falling endlessly to I don't know where,
fearful to of what is there!
Shivering, dithering, colder than ice,
fearful of where its taking my life.
Trying to be strong, strong and robust
as its all that I have - I know it's a must.
Tiring me, hurting me, I fall to my knees....
is this my life?...no please, please, please.

I try to walk but can only crawl,
I try to shout!!..but there's nothing at all,
I'm tired now my strength has gone,
tears fall...my body's done.
I need to sleep, I need to rest,

I'm really tired....I've done my best.
I hope tomorrow, when I sleep again
that the journey is different...and there's little pain
I hope to learn quickly and fast...
as this is just my first night...and it won't be my last!

Faces

Who do I ask for forgiveness
and how is it that I ask?
Do I beg and crawl, across the floors?
Who is it that I ask?
For I have sinned a lifetime,
hurt those that crossed my path.
Will I have to spend my next lifetime,
trying to pay it back?

Although I'm strong, I've done wrong,
And I need forgiveness to help my path.
See, I can go forth no more,
I'm only going back.
I've walked my life blindfolded,
yet I can clearly see.
But pain and grief, is what I see,
will forgiveness ever come for me?

At night when I close my eyes,
distorted faces that I see.
Of all those I've hurt, changed lives for the worst...
...all because of me.
I know I can't move on like this,

every day it brings me pain
And crying every single night...
...again, again, again!

But forgiveness is not forth coming,
but my tears they gladly will.
And every night, just like last night visit me,
they surely will.
So punishment this is for me,
no forgiveness will come my way.
And I will see their faces, and cry for ever more,
And no sleep will come, for all I've done,
to those with distorted faces.

Your Eyes

Please forgive me the best you can,
please try to forget what was bad, if you can.
Though surely you have suffered and cried a stream,
and immensely you were tortured
at the hands of your dream,
and I try to understand it, search for reasons why,
I try to figure out all the wrongs I supply.

But it's not that I don't love you, and care nothing at all,
it's not that I don't need you, or want you at all,
but I will make no excuses try to cover it with lies,
and it will never be justified
what you saw through your eyes.

And I wish that I could change things, I really wish I could,
as you deserve so much more
for your desire, faith and love,
but time is the only healer for the way you've had to live
and I know you deserve much more,
much more than I can give.

So reluctantly I release you, so hard to let you go,
reluctantly I'll break your chains,
so to allow for you to grow,

and all though I know I'll miss you
and it will tear my soul apart,
I know the time has come
to give a better man your heart.

Skin deep

For brave is the courage of man,
to let fear of love, choose his steps,
to be strong for all around of him,
to lead and bring courage to others.
To cry silently, and parade a smile,
which hides true feelings from his way to give,
for those that are weaker, grow stronger,
for what they see him give.

There's no piercing of his armour,
from the outside in,
and he will be brave and strong,
no matter how helpless this time may be.
And he will move forward and walk over his fellow man,
who fall at his feet,
and breath their last breath,
and he will continue to move forward.

And be courageous, with every step he takes...
...and knowing he may not see the light of day again.
But to sacrifice he must so those that follow,
embrace the strength of man,
and what their willing to give,

for the sake of those that follow,
to camouflage from fearing eyes,
the reality of pain and sorrow,
until such time, they can walk alone.

Because his strength, that blankets those that follow,
will one day grow old and whither,
and no longer will his strength be enough
But now they should be so much stronger,
and others will now follow them, and they,
will guide and lead, and be courageous along the way,
and they will have their own disguise,
so those that follow, do not fear the day.

Segregated

Segregated, pushed aside
living my life in an invisible domain.
Every door that opens another one slams.
Hearing everything all around
but they don't hear me, not at all, not a sound.
Trying to do what I think is right,
trying to abide with the laws of this life.
But to me it's different within this domain,
the laws that are there mine alone.
Trying to move forward, my life to begin,
trying to live like you, like him.
But in this domain, my place, my home...
only I look out, you can all look in.

Day trip

So young and innocent to be taken,
when stories of life were yet to be learnt,
to feel one feeling that you will never feel again,
and to cry so many tears.

To fear all those that are near you,
though they know your name,
you do not know theirs, to listen to their comforting words,
but not to know what you're listening to at all.

To not to sleep with strangers around you,
as your kin usually slept by your side,
to listen to whimpering of children's sad journey,
as tiredness as made them sleep and dream.

To have no understanding of what's around you,
to fear the hands that feed your mouth,
to keep walking to you don't know where,
to hide away and sob to your own story, in this place, that
you don't know where.

To leave, run, escape you think,
but you have no idea where you are,
to stand in the middle of nowhere, to be lost,

but you don't know where,
to walk on into the darkness, as you'd rather be fearful
here, than petrified there.

To shivering, but it makes you become stronger,
as you only have yourself that you can trust,
but a child is all you are,
and to be frightened you always must.

As an adult, that I now become,
the dreams they still remain,
I still have shivering, and become frightened,
and the children's dream's they come the same.

And the hands that tried to feed me,
and the comforting words that never came,
I still remember this every day,
and I still don't know their names.

Monster

Go away leave my mind you were not asked to be here.
Your poison and vermin like the deadliest snake,
you force me to hunger you,
to be part of my life
and all that you bring is trouble and strife.

You choose the vulnerable, the lost and the weak...
then rip them apart, though they were sheets.
You stay with them constantly
through day and night,
taking over their consciousness, leading their lives.

And when you have violated them,
dragged them to their lowest point
you abandoned their minds
so they come begging at your feet,
enjoying every moment....to you it's a treat!

And for those that overcome you,
manage to tear their souls away,
they're left there with nothing, no will to survive.
For you: your work is finished...
there's many more for you to thrive.

Patches

Far away a distant past it seems,
of when I was just a boy.
To skip of school, and break some rules -
help the milk man for the day.
My half-masts were a sad old sight,
my shoes - footie boots with no studs!
My t-shirt - one of the Muppets,
the one that played the drums!

For hours I would skip around,
beneath a friendly sun,
And not a worry I would have,
and not a worry to anyone.
I'd walk amongst the pine trees,
maybe climb an oak.
Or just sit there and listen,
to the magpies laugh and joke.

I'd light a little campfire,
cook my bacon on a spade.
Then sit and think, and look around,
and wonder how this earth was made.
I'd think of running away from home

and build a log cabin in the woods.
To live off the land would be my plans,
though I was just a lad.

But the cold would tickle my fingers,
the winds would say I'm mad.
And the creatures that were spying on me,
would scare me something bad.
So off I'd trot to the comfort,
of the coal shed in our yard,
to stuff my face with coal like lace.
Until tomorrow again it starts.

Happier Song

Feeling sad, feeling down
my face gives nothing but a frown.
Wanting to leave here wanting to go,
wanting to resume life as I know.
Feeling desperate, I often do -
feeling sorry for me...not you!

But I have wronged you, and for that I must pay...
but is this really the only way!
Many will suffer, many will cry,
and then to ask for reasons why.
Acceptance is my path now, responsibility is mine,
I have to walk this path alone, no matter how much time.

And when my path has ended
and my soul redeems what's wrong,
I may walk with you,
hand in hand...
to a happier song.

Touch

Bleed my soul for its kindness,
take my hands for their cold.
Look in for my rich desires,
as time comes to make me old.

Caress me how you think you should,
hold me tight as I grow cold.
Kiss my brow and stroke my hair,
so I know your love is there.

Hold me tighter and closer,
as I fear that I may fall.
Keep me by your side my love,
wipe my sadness as it calls.

My body is a lonely one,
it needs to have your touch.
Your are the one it's calling too,
it wants you oh so much.

I fear that I may find myself,
somewhere that you can't find.
With no passion, understanding
or love of any kind.

Where all walk a sorry stroll,
mumbled words that make no rhyme.
To be punished and be stranded here,
where there's no such thing as time.

Without you here to comfort me,
feed me strength so I survive,
my body will quickly age my love
and my departure before its time.

So I hold on to you tightly,
to release would be my sin,
and that place that's so fearful for me,
that place I've never been,
will send its soldiers for my soul,
and a cruel afterlife begin.

Along The Way

Lying here waiting, wishing you here,
wanting you closer, wanting you near.
Your hair upon my skin, your comforts to my ears
wanting to let you know,
I just needed a little help along the way.
Just a little help along the way.

When I'm trying to find my feet, the path, the way,
when I'm trying to find the reasons, how do I say:
I just needed a little help along the way,
just a little help along the way.

When I try to touch my children,
when I want to stay and play.
When I try to reach out to them
seems harder every day.
I just needed a little help along the way,
just a little help along the way.

I wish I could thank my mother,
I wish I could show I cared,
I wish I could make her understand
that I know that she is there.

I just needed some help along the way,
just a little help along the way.

When my time in life is over
or our paths take different ways
or love comes knocking at your door
to give you better days.
Remember that I loved you,
remember that I cared
and remember deep in your heart
so much pain you're kindly spared.
I just needed some help along the way,
just a little help along the way.

Campfire Nights

Campfire smoke - like sand in my eyes,
a giggle, a laughter at some poor soul's lies.
Talking of what we will do from tomorrow,
"that's what I'm doing", "its decided", "it's time".
Light another cigarette - maybe a toke,
sit there and listen, give the campfire a poke.
Stand up and wonder, look to the sky,
ask for the answers to your troubles, your cries.
Sit there and think, crack a small smile,
then gently retreat to your conscience, your hole.
Then reach for your saviour, it's all in your world,
respect it, accept it, stand up and walk tall.
Realise there are times that everybody falls,
gaze into your campfire, drift a million miles away
then fall back to reality as the flames they start to play.
Cry a little longer, wipe your runny nose,
then to lie down gracefully smile towards your friends,
then drift off slowly, slowly fall to sleep,
these campfire nights are the best and they're for keeps.

Pretty Once

She invites me into her ancient house, with the flash of
smile from her stained brown teeth.
The room is warm from the open fire, candlesticks flicker
leaving their signature upon the walls.
I sit at a window gazing out, but my view is hampered from
the tear in my eye and from the cracks in the
window and the elements of wind
creeping in through its rotten frame.

"I was pretty once!" she turns and says.
I look at her gracefully, all the contours of her face, worn
and drawn like tissue to the bone...the face of a
million disappointments and many years of hope.
"My husband was a gentle man...worked his hands to the
bone - built this very house".
" Where is he now"?, I asked.
She looks at me, as if to stare as she knows that I know,
that he has long since passed.

"What brings you here, to this part of the woods?"
I pause, having to think and not really knowing why.
"You lost? Lost my child?"
"No. I'm not lost - I live round here"

As she offers me some soup, again, I am speechless.

"You should finish your soup and be on your way,

it will be dark soon".

I finish my soup, thank her and walk to the door.

"Stick to the path my child and soon you will be home"

As I leave, she calls to me and I turn and listen.

"I was pretty once you know".

I smile and leave.

Cleave, Cleave!...Are you alright?

"Oh yes, I'm fine"

"Thought I'd lost you there for a minute! We'd better go - it

will be dark soon".

"How many of them mushrooms did you have anyway?".

Corridors

Lets walk together down these corridors of life,
hand in hand, let's talk not fight.
Talk of your secrets, thoughts, desire,
talk of all things that reach out and inspire.

This night is ours, and ours alone
all is dark but you that glows.
Talk and I will listen, I will read your mind -
who knows what is there and what I will find.

Your eyes are your secrets,
the gates to your mind,
I will find what is there,
what joy's do you hide?

Is there corridors deep in your mind,
doors with no keys, for no one to find.
Happiness, sadness, love and hate;
all behind doors or big iron gates.

Let me in, let me wonder in this world of your own,
to walk along side you, or to carry you if I must,
to be there beside you, to be right by your side
this place of wonder....the sanctuary of your mind.

Place Of Wonder

Strange places of wonder, many riches to find,
much happiness and laughter -
such amazement to one's eyes.
No money is spent here, it really doesn't exist,
nothing expensive - everyone's rich.
Children they play here and sleep well at night,
nothing to fear here, nothing to fright.
They know nothing of monsters, ghouls and ghosts
but everything of Santa and Easter bunnies alike.
Elfins and fairy's they're the children's best friends,
no one is lonely everyone's friends.
Nobody fights here, nobody shouts.
Moms and Dads stay together,
brothers and sisters don't fall out.
All greetings come with smiles kisses and hugs,
and everyone does what one really loves.
Everyone's pleasant here and really so kind,
where is this place?...buried deep in one's mind.

Crying Sky

The sound of thunder - the pale blue sky,
just wanting to burst just wanting to cry.
Tears of many, anger of all,
just wanting to spill just wanting to fall.
All life is kept there all emotion and pain,
all feelings and anger fall as snow and the rain.

Rivers get polluted from anger and pain,
and nothing at all grows because of our shame!
And all our emotions have scorched all the Plains,
the wind burns your ears from the lies and the tales.
All the ancients are naked from violence and hate,
prevented from growing because of this place.

When our eyes they dance over this vast landscape
they bleed from the shame for our moral disgrace.
This land was pleasure for all to share,
but we raped it and burnt it without any care...
and now we are losing it, watching it die.
Why? The crying sky.

Protector

Sit here besides me, down by my side,
there's nothing to fear we have nothing to hide.
I am your keeper, your god, your saint,
all that you love and all that you hate.
I am the cause of your dreams and your faith.
I am your creation, your breath your blood,
and all that is bad and all that is good,
all that you wanted and all that you need,
I am the person that carries and leads.

I'll do as you ask me, your servant I'll be,
for here ever after and forever to be.
If you're hurt - I will heal you.
When you're hungry - I'll feed.
If confronted by madness, insanity or death,
I'll fight for your liberty your innocence, your love,
I'll fight all the gods from the heavens above.
I am your protector, to defend you is my goal
and if I was to fail...to be punished until old.

Tick-Tock

To find passage that I wander,
to find gates that crumble in my hands,
to make reasons that make no guide to me,
as I wander to be found.

I strolled upon a delicate ground,
every step that takes a breath,
the thumping of my inner soul,
echoes a different text.

I ride upon the wings of time -
tick-tock, tick-tock, it stops -
to ride again, it carries me
a decade of time has passed.

Too slow, too fast, I wander,
I learn through the passage of time -
tick-tock, tick-tock it's stopped again,
as time becomes my master.

I stop, I halt, I have to think,
but too much streams my way,
a waterfall of knowledge cascading down my way -
tick-tock, tick-tock it's stopped again.

I stand on rotten wood,

there's cracks in all my honesty.

I walk on sodden mud, I turn, I stop,

I run away, though there's nothing below my feet.

I bleed, I burn, I cry,

I scream along these ticking streets...

tick-tock, tick-tock it's stopped again,

tick-tock, tick-tock it's stopped.

Acknowledgements:

A massive thank you to everyone who has liked, commented and shared my poems on Facebook over the last year. To Lee, who not only prompted me to get this project off the ground, but also helped along the way and eventually ended up being the photographer as well! To Freddie, for being my cover star and to my Helentree, for her unwavering support and unending patience as my editor and ultimately my publisher. I couldn't have done this without the help and support you have all given me, without you there would not be this - CLEAVE x